TELEPATHY

TELEPATHY

THE SILENT LANGUAGE OF UNIVERSE

Dr.A.K.Saxena, Ph.D.

**Copyright © 2024
Dr.A.K.Saxena, Ph.D.**

All rights reserved. no part of this publication may be reproduced, recorded for purpose of retrieval, or transmitted in any form or by any means, including photocopying, recording, or any other electronic or mechanical methods, except in the case of brief quotations embodied in critical reviews and certain other non-commercial uses permitted by the copyright law.

TABLE OF CONTENTS

Preface

1. Introduction
2. The Mysterious World of Telepathy
3. Historical Perspectives on Telepathy in Different Cultures
4. The Neuroscience of Telepathy
5. The Physics of Telepathy
6. Intuitive Telepathy
7. Emotional Telepathy

8. Mental Telepathy
9. Astral Telepathy
10. Telepathy in Relationships
11. Telepathy in Business Relationships
12. Telepathy in Healing and Therapy
13. Some Real-life Examples of Telepathy in Daily Life
14. The Evolution of Human Consciousness
15. Developing Telepathic Abilities

16. The Role of Intuition in Telepathy
17. Telepathy and the Universe
18. The Ethics of Telepathy
19. Telepathic Communication in the Future
20. The Global Implications of Telepathy
21. Unlocking the Full Potential of Telepathy
22. The Epilogue
23. Further Reading

@@@@

PREFACE

"Mind-meld, Doctor?" - Mr. Spock

"No, no, no! Not now, Spock! I'am trying to break the telepathic connection!" - Dr. Leonard "Bones" McCoy

Do you recall this quote from the classic sci-fi movie *"Star Trek IV: The Voyage Home"* (1986)? The quote highlights the Vulcan mind-meld, a telepathic technique used by Vulcans to share thoughts and ideas directly.

In an age where technology connects us in ways previously unimaginable, the exploration of telepathy—communication
beyond the spoken word—invites us to ponder the depths of human potential. This book delves into the fascinating realm of telepathy,

examining its historical roots, scientific inquiries, and cultural interpretations.

Telepathy, often dismissed as mere fantasy, has captivated the minds of thinkers, scientists, and storytellers alike. From ancient philosophies to modern psychological studies, the concept challenges our understanding of consciousness and the interconnectedness of all beings. As we navigate through the chapters, we will uncover the significance of telepathy not only as a phenomenon but also as a potential catalyst for empathy, understanding, and unity in an increasingly fragmented world.

By bridging the gap between the known and the unknown, this book aims to inspire curiosity and open-mindedness. It invites readers to explore the possibilities that lie within our minds and the profound implications of truly connecting with one another. Whether you are a skeptic, a believer, or simply a curious soul, join us on this journey into the extraordinary world of telepathy, where the boundaries of communication expand, and the essence of human experience is redefined.

@@@@

CHAPTER 1

INTRODUCTION

Telepathy, the ability to communicate without words or physical cues, has long been a subject of fascination and curiosity for many. From science fiction novels to ancient myths and legends, it has captured the imagination of people across cultures and time periods. But what if I tell you that telepathy is not just a figment of our imagination or a product of science fiction, but a very real and innate ability that we all possess? My book, *"Telepathy: The Silent Language of the Universe,"* aims to shed light on this powerful phenomenon and uncover its secrets.

The concept of telepathy has been around for centuries, with evidence of its existence found in various cultures and religions. In ancient Greek mythology, *Hermes*, the messenger god, was believed to possess telepathic abilities. In Hinduism, telepathy is referred to as *"manasa-gamana,"* which translates to *"mind movement."* Even in modern times, numerous studies have been conducted to explore the possibility of telepathy, with some yielding promising results.

So what exactly is telepathy? Simply put, it is the transfer of thoughts, feelings, or sensations between individuals without any verbal or physical communication. This exchange can occur between two people who are in close proximity or even when they are miles apart. It is often referred to as the silent language of the universe because it transcends the barriers of language and distance.

In my book, I delve into the different forms of telepathy and how they manifest in our lives. The first form is instinctual telepathy, which is commonly referred to as intuition. We have all experienced moments when we just knew something without any logical explanation. This is our instinctual telepathic ability at play. It is our primal survival instinct that allows us to sense potential danger or connect with others on a deeper level.

The second form is mental telepathy, which involves the transmission of thoughts and ideas between two or more individuals. It is often associated with twin siblings or close friends who seem to have a strong connection and can communicate without speaking a word. Mental telepathy is not limited to just humans; it also exists in the animal kingdom. Animals, such as dolphins and wolves, use telepathy to communicate with one another and coordinate their actions.

The third form is emotional telepathy, which involves the transfer of emotions between individuals. This is why we can sometimes feel the emotions of those around us, even if they do not express them verbally. For example, have you ever walked into a room and immediately sensed tension or joy? That is emotional telepathy at work.

The fourth and most advanced form is astral telepathy. It

involves the transfer of thoughts and ideas between individuals who are in different states of consciousness. This can happen during meditation, lucid dreaming, or astral projection. It allows us to tap into a higher level of consciousness and connect with others on a spiritual level.

But how does telepathy actually work? The exact mechanism behind it is still a mystery, but there are several theories that attempt to explain it. One theory suggests that telepathy works through the transmission of electromagnetic waves between individuals. Another theory proposes that it is based on quantum entanglement, where particles are connected regardless of distance and can influence each other's behavior.

Regardless of the mechanism behind it, there is no denying the existence and power of telepathy.

In my book, I provide real-life examples and studies that support its existence. From twins who can sense each other's emotions from miles away to experiments where individuals were able to accurately transmit images and words to each other, the evidence is compelling.

But why is this ability so important? Why do we need to explore and understand telepathy? The answer lies in its potential to bring humanity closer together. In a world where language barriers, cultural differences, and physical distance often hinder communication, telepathy has the power to bridge those gaps. It can help us understand each other on a deeper level and foster empathy and compassion.

Moreover, telepathy has the potential to unlock the secrets of the universe. By tapping into a higher level of consciousness, we can access information and knowledge beyond what our physical senses can perceive. This can lead to groundbreaking discoveries and advancements in science and technology.

In conclusion, my book, *"Telepathy: The Silent Language of the Universe,"* is a comprehensive and detailed introduction to the powerful phenomenon of telepathy. It explores its different forms, provides evidence of its existence, and discusses its potential impact on our lives and society. I hope that it will not only satisfy the curiosity of those who are interested in this subject but also inspire others to unlock their own telepathic abilities and harness its power for the betterment of humanity. After all, as the saying goes, *"thoughts become things,"* and telepathy is the ultimate tool for manifesting our desires.

@@@@

CHAPTER 2

THE MYSTERIOUS WORLD OF TELEPATHY

Telepathy, often referred to as mind-to-mind communication, is a mysterious and elusive concept that has captured the imaginations of humans for centuries. It is the ability to communicate and transfer thoughts, feelings, or sensations between two individuals without any physical connection. Some view it as a supernatural power, while others believe it to be a scientific phenomenon that is yet to be fully understood. Regardless of personal beliefs, the concept of telepathy continues to fascinate and intrigue people all around the world.

The Origin of Telepathy:

The concept of telepathy dates back to ancient civilizations, where it was believed that certain individuals possessed the ability to communicate through their minds. In Greek mythology, Hermes was the messenger god who had the power of telepathy, and in Hindu mythology, Lord Krishna was known for his telepathic abilities. The concept also appears in various religious texts and spiritual traditions, often associated with psychic abilities and supernatural powers.

In modern times, telepathy gained popularity during the late 19th century with the emergence of spiritualism. Spiritualists believed that telepathy was a form of mediumship through which spirits could communicate with the living. However, with the rise of scientific inquiry and skepticism in the 20th century, telepathy was dismissed as a mere superstition and relegated to the realm of pseudoscience.

The Science Behind Telepathy:

Despite its controversial history, many scientists and researchers continue to study telepathy in hopes of understanding its underlying mechanisms. One theory is that telepathic communication occurs through electromagnetic waves emitted by the brain. These waves are thought to contain information that can be transferred from one individual to another through a receiver's brain.

Another theory suggests that telepathic communication is based on quantum entanglement, where two particles become connected in such a way that the state of one particle can affect the state of the other, regardless of the distance between them. This theory proposes that telepathy is a form of non-local communication that operates outside of our traditional understanding of time and space.

The Evidence for Telepathy:

Despite being dismissed by many as pseudoscience, there have been several well-documented cases of telepathy that have left scientists and researchers baffled. One of the most famous examples is the case of Lulu and Willy, a set of twins who were separated at birth but were able to communicate telepathically with each other. They could accurately predict each other's thoughts and feelings, even when they were physically apart.

In another study conducted in 2014, researchers at Bangor University in Wales found evidence of telepathic communication between two participants who were placed in separate rooms. The participants were asked to interact with each other through a computer interface, but unknown to them, the experiment was rigged so that one participant could send messages to the other using only their thoughts. The results showed a significantly higher success rate than would be expected by chance, indicating some form of telepathic communication between the two participants.

Exploring Telepathy's Potential:

The concept of telepathy has also piqued the interest of many futurists and technology enthusiasts who believe that it has the potential to revolutionize human communication. With advancements in technology, such as brain-computer interfaces, there is growing speculation about the possibility of developing devices that can facilitate telepathic communication between individuals.

Some experts even suggest that telepathy could be used to enhance human capabilities, allowing us to access information and communicate with each other instantaneously without the need for language or physical gestures. This has raised ethical concerns about privacy and control over one's thoughts in a world where telepathy is a reality.

The Limits of Telepathy:

While there may be evidence to support the existence of telepathy, there is also a lack of concrete scientific evidence to prove its validity. The experiments conducted so far have been criticized for their small sample sizes and the possibility of fraud or chance outcomes. Additionally, even if telepathy does exist, it may be limited to certain individuals or situations, making it difficult to study and replicate.

Moreover, our brains are complex organs, and it is still not fully understood how they work. It is possible that what we perceive as telepathy could simply be a result of our brains processing and interpreting information in a way that appears telepathic. Without a solid understanding of the brain and its capabilities, it is challenging to definitively say whether telepathy exists or not.

The Future of Telepathy:

With ongoing research and advancements in technology, the concept of telepathy may become less mysterious and more scientifically understood in the future. It has already sparked interesting discussions about the nature of consciousness, the limits of human perception, and the potential for human evolution.

However, whether telepathy is a supernatural power or a scientific phenomenon, one thing is for sure - it continues to capture our curiosity and imagination. The allure of being able to communicate with someone without speaking a single word is a fascinating concept that has propelled us to explore its mysteries. And as we continue on this journey of discovery, perhaps one day, we will unlock the secrets of telepathy and unravel its enigma once and for all.

The world of telepathy remains an enigma, with much yet to be discovered and understood. Whether it is a supernatural power or a scientific phenomenon, one thing is certain - it has captured our fascination and will continue to do so for years to come. Who knows what the future holds for this mysterious form of communication? Only time will tell.

@@@@

CHAPTER 3

HISTORICAL PERSPECTIVES ON

TELEPATHY IN DIFFERENT CULTURES

Telepathy, also known as mind-to-mind communication, is the ability to transmit thoughts and information from one person to another without the use of any physical means. This phenomenon has been a subject of fascination and curiosity for centuries, appearing in various forms in different cultures around the world. From ancient myths and legends to modern-day scientific studies, telepathy has captured the imagination of people across cultures and continues to be a topic of interest.

To truly understand the concept of telepathy, it is essential to explore its historical perspectives in different cultures. This not only sheds light on the evolution of this phenomenon but also provides a glimpse into how it has been perceived and used by different societies. So let's take a journey through time and dive into the fascinating history of telepathy in different cultures.

Ancient Egypt: The Birthplace of Telepathy?

The roots of telepathy can be traced back to ancient Egypt, where it was believed to be a gift from the gods. The ancient Egyptians had a strong belief in the afterlife and that communication between the living and the dead was possible through telepathy. The Book of the Dead, an ancient Egyptian funerary text, contains spells and incantations that were thought to help the deceased communicate with the living using telepathy.

In addition, hieroglyphs found in temples and tombs depict images of individuals communicating through mental means, further reinforcing the belief in telepathy.

It is also interesting to note that the Egyptian god Thoth was believed to be the god of telepathy and communication.

Ancient Greece: The Influence of Mythology

The ancient Greeks also had a strong belief in telepathy, which was heavily influenced by their mythology. In Greek mythology, Hermes, the messenger god, was also considered the god of telepathy and was believed to be capable of communicating telepathically with other gods and mortals.

The Greek philosopher, Aristotle, also wrote about telepathy in his works. He believed that the mind could emit and receive energy, which could be used for telepathic communication. This idea of a universal energy connecting all living beings has been a common thread in many cultures and is still prevalent in modern-day theories about telepathy.

Native American Cultures: The Power of Intuition

Many Native American tribes and cultures have a strong belief in telepathy and consider it to be an innate ability of the human mind. In these cultures, telepathy is seen as a form of intuition or sixth sense, which allows individuals to communicate with each other without the need for words.

The Navajo tribe, for instance, has a concept known as *"skinwalkers,"* who are believed to possess the ability to communicate telepathically with others and even shape-shift into animals. The Hopi tribe also has a similar belief and uses telepathy as a means of communication during rituals and ceremonies.

Eastern Cultures: Yogic Powers and Psychic Abilities

In many Eastern cultures, such as Hinduism and Buddhism, telepathy is seen as one of the siddhis or supernatural powers attained through meditation and spiritual practices. These cultures believe that through meditation and yogic practices, one can develop psychic abilities, including telepathy.

In Hinduism, there is a concept known as *"samadhi,"* which is said to be a state of complete concentration and oneness with the universe. In this state, it is believed that one can communicate with others telepathically and even gain knowledge about past, present, and future events.

Modern-Day Perspectives: From Parapsychology to Scientific Studies

In the 19th century, the term *"telepathy"* was coined by the famous British researcher Frederic W.H. Myers, who conducted extensive studies on the subject along with other pioneers of parapsychology. These studies focused on the possibility of telepathic communication between individuals and explored its potential uses in various fields, such as medicine and law enforcement.

In the 20th century, telepathy gained even more attention with the rise of science and technology. Scientists began conducting experiments to test the validity of telepathy and its potential as a means of communication. While some studies have shown promising results, telepathy remains a controversial topic in the scientific community.

The Role of Culture in Shaping Perspectives on Telepathy

The different cultural beliefs and practices surrounding telepathy provide a fascinating insight into how this phenomenon has been perceived and used throughout history. While some cultures view it as a supernatural ability or a gift from the gods, others see it as a natural aspect of human intuition or a product of intense spiritual practices.

Furthermore, cultural beliefs and practices have also influenced the ways in which telepathy has been studied and researched. In some cultures, it is accepted as a legitimate means of communication, while in others, it is met with skepticism and doubt.

The history of telepathy in different cultures highlights the enduring fascination with this phenomenon and its potential uses. From ancient civilizations to modern-day scientific studies, telepathy remains a topic of interest and continues to spark debates and discussions about its existence and validity.

While there is still much to be explored and understood about telepathy, one thing is certain –

its potential for communication and connection has captured the imagination of people across cultures for centuries. Whether through myths and legends or scientific studies, the concept of mind-to-mind communication continues to intrigue us, leaving us to wonder about the endless possibilities of this mysterious phenomenon.

@@@@

CHAPTER 4

THE NEUROSCIENCE OF TELEPATHY

Telepathy, the ability to communicate with others through thoughts and feelings without any physical interactions, has been a subject of fascination for centuries. From science fiction novels to paranormal claims, the concept of mind-to-mind communication has captured our imaginations. But what if I told you that telepathy may not just be a myth or a supernatural phenomenon, but something rooted in the science of our brains?

The study of telepathy falls under the realm of parapsychology, which is the scientific investigation of paranormal and psychic phenomena. However, in recent years, there has been an increasing interest in understanding telepathy from a neurological perspective. Researchers are now exploring the brain mechanisms that may be involved in this fascinating ability.

So, let's dive into the world of telepathy and explore the neuroscience behind it.

What is Telepathy?

Telepathy is derived from the Greek words *"tele,"* meaning distant, and *"pathos,"* meaning feeling or perception. It is commonly defined as the communication between individuals through thoughts and feelings without any known physical means of transmission.

The concept of telepathy can be traced back to ancient times, with references in Hindu, Buddhist, and Greek mythology. In the 19th century, it gained more attention with the rise of spiritualism and mediumship. However, it was only in the 20th century that telepathy started to be studied scientifically.

The Science Behind Telepathy

The human brain is a complex organ capable of remarkable feats. It is responsible for all our thoughts, feelings, and actions.

But can it also enable us to communicate with each other without speaking or using any other form of communication? The scientific community has been divided on this question for decades.

According to a study published in the journal Neuroscience & Biobehavioral Reviews, telepathy can be explained by the phenomenon of *"mind-reading."* It is the ability to understand and interpret someone else's thoughts and emotions through non-verbal cues, such as body language and facial expressions. This can happen even without any conscious awareness on the part of the sender or receiver.

Another theory suggests that telepathy may be a result of synchronicity in brain activity between two individuals. This means that when two people are in close proximity, their brains may produce similar patterns of electrical activity, leading to *"mental resonance,"* which allows them to share thoughts and emotions.

The Role of Mirror Neurons

One of the most prominent theories in the neuroscience of telepathy is the role of mirror neurons. These neurons are a specialized type of brain cell that fires when an individual performs an action or observes someone else performing the same action. They are responsible for empathy and imitation, which are essential for social behavior and communication.

A study published in the journal Cognitive Neuroscience found that mirror neurons may play a crucial role in telepathic communication. The researchers used *functional magnetic resonance imaging (fMRI)* to observe brain activity in participants who were asked to communicate non-verbally with each other. They found that when one participant sent a message, their mirror neurons would fire, and the receiver's mirror neurons would also activate, creating a shared neural representation of the message.

The Power of Intention

Intention is another important factor in the neuroscience of telepathy. Our intentions are reflected in our thoughts, emotions, and actions, and they can act as a powerful force in shaping our reality. Studies have shown that focused mental intention can influence physical events and even alter brain activity.

In a study published in the journal PNAS, researchers found

that individuals who were asked to focus their intentions on a specific location were able to influence random number generators placed at that location. This suggests that our intentions can have a direct impact on the physical world.

The Potential Applications of Telepathy

While telepathy may seem like something out of a science fiction novel, it has the potential to have significant practical applications. For example, telepathic communication can be used to help individuals with speech and communication disorders, such as aphasia or autism. It can also be used in therapeutic settings to improve emotional understanding and empathy between individuals.

Telepathic communication can also have practical uses in military and emergency response situations, where verbal communication may not be possible or efficient. It can also aid in covert operations and espionage.

The Limitations and Controversies

Despite the progress made in understanding the neuroscience of telepathy, there are still many limitations and controversies surrounding its validity. Skeptics argue that there is no scientific evidence to support telepathy, and that any apparent instances of telepathic communication can be explained by other factors, such as coincidence or cold reading.

Moreover, there is still much debate on the mechanisms behind telepathy and whether it can be learned or controlled. While some believe that telepathy may be an innate ability that can be enhanced through training, others argue that it may be a random occurrence with no control over it.

The study of telepathy from a neurological perspective is still in its infancy, and there is much more research to be done. While some may view it as a pseudoscience or a supernatural ability, the emerging scientific evidence suggests that telepathy may have a basis in the functioning of our brains.

The idea of being able to communicate with others through our thoughts and emotions is both intriguing and daunting. The neuroscience behind telepathy opens up a whole new world of possibilities and challenges our understanding of human connection. Who knows what the future holds for this elusive phenomenon, but one thing is for sure: the study of telepathy will continue to captivate our minds for years to come.

@@@@

CHAPTER 5

THE PHYSICS OF TELEPATHY

Telepathy, the concept of communicating with another person's thoughts without the use of spoken or written language, has long been a subject of fascination and speculation. From science fiction novels to psychic readings, the idea of mind-to-mind communication has always captured our imagination. But is telepathy just a product of our imagination or is there a scientific explanation for it? In this chapter, we will dive into the physics behind telepathy and explore the fascinating science behind this mysterious phenomenon.

The Physics of Telepathy

To understand the physics behind telepathy, we must first define what telepathy actually is. According to parapsychologists, telepathy is defined as the ability to sense or transmit thoughts, feelings, or mental images from one person to another without the use of any known medium or physical interaction. This means that telepathy involves the transmission and reception of information without any apparent physical connection between two individuals.

The concept of telepathy is closely linked to the properties of energy and how it can be transmitted from one source to another. In physics, energy is defined as the ability to do work or cause change. It exists in different forms such as light, heat, sound, and electromagnetic waves. These forms of energy can be transmitted through various mediums such as air, water, and even empty space.

According to some scientists, telepathy could be a form of energy transmission that we have yet to fully understand. Just like how radio waves can transmit information from one location to another through space, it is possible that telepathy works in a similar manner. In this case, the human brain could act as a transmitter and receiver of this energy.

The Human Brain and Telepathy

The human brain is a complex network of neurons and electrical signals that constantly communicate with each other. These electrical signals are produced by the movement of ions within the brain cells and are essential for various brain functions such as thinking, feeling, and sensing. Scientists have discovered that these electrical signals can also travel outside the body and interact with other brains in close proximity.

In a 2014 study published in the journal *PLOS ONE*, researchers from Duke University found evidence that human brains can communicate with each other through electromagnetic signals.

The study involved two participants who were hooked up to EEG machines that measured their brain activity. The participants were then asked to play a game where they had to cooperate with each other to win. The results showed that their brain waves synchronized and communicated with each other, even when there was no physical interaction between them.

This study suggests that telepathy could be a result of brain-to-brain communication through electromagnetic waves. The human brain produces a range of electromagnetic frequencies, from low-frequency delta waves to high-frequency beta waves. These frequencies are constantly fluctuating depending on our thoughts, emotions, and actions.

In another study published in the journal Scientific Reports, researchers found that people who claimed to have telepathic abilities had significantly higher levels of low-frequency theta and alpha waves in their brains compared to those who did not have such abilities. These waves are associated with a relaxed and receptive state of mind, which could make it easier for them to pick up and send telepathic signals.

The Quantum Connection

Apart from electromagnetic waves, some scientists believe that quantum mechanics could also play a role in telepathy. According to quantum theory, particles can be connected in a state called *"quantum entanglement,"* where any change to one particle will immediately affect the other, no matter how far apart they are. This phenomenon has been observed in particles of light and has been proven to exist in the subatomic world.

Some scientists believe that this same principle could also apply to the human brain and its ability to communicate telepathically. In a 2014 study published in the journal PLOS ONE, researchers from the University of British Columbia found that two minds can be connected in a state of quantum entanglement when they are in close proximity. This could explain how telepathy works, as the sender and receiver's brains could be entangled, allowing for the transmission of thoughts and feelings.

The Limits of Telepathy

While there is evidence to suggest that telepathy could be a real phenomenon, it is important to note that there are still many unknowns and limitations. The human brain is a complex and mysterious organ, and we have yet to fully understand its capabilities.

Additionally, many claimed instances of telepathy have been debunked as coincidences or misinterpretations. It is crucial to approach the study of telepathy with a critical and scientific mindset to avoid falling into the trap of pseudoscience.

In conclusion, the physics behind telepathy is still a subject of ongoing research and debate. While there is some evidence to suggest that telepathy could be a real phenomenon, more studies are needed to fully understand its mechanics and limitations. The human brain is a powerful organ with many mysteries waiting to be unlocked, and perhaps one day we will have a better understanding of the fascinating science behind telepathy. Until then, let our imaginations run wild and continue to explore the wonders of the mind.

@@@@

CHAPTER 6

INTUITIVE TELEPATHY

When we think about communication, we often think about words. We use spoken or written language to convey our thoughts, feelings, and ideas to others. But what if we told you that there is another form of communication that goes beyond words and language? A form of communication that transcends physical barriers and can connect us with others on a deeper level. That form is known as intuitive telepathy.

Intuitive telepathy, also known as intercommunication or mind-to-mind communication, is the ability to communicate with others through thoughts, feelings, and emotions without the use of words. It is often seen as a form of *extrasensory perception (ESP)* and has been a subject of fascination for centuries.

The concept of telepathy has been mentioned in ancient texts and mythology, with stories of people being able to communicate telepathically with animals, plants, and even the spirit world. However, it wasn't until the late 19th century that the term "telepathy" was coined by psychologist Frederic Myers. He defined it as the ability to transfer thoughts or feelings from one mind to another without the use of the senses.

Since then, scientific research on intuitive telepathy has been ongoing. While there is still much debate among scientists and researchers about its existence and validity, there have been numerous studies that suggest its potential and benefits.

So how exactly does intuitive telepathy work? It is believed that this form of communication is possible due to the human brain's ability to emit and receive electromagnetic waves. Every thought or emotion we have creates an electrical impulse in our brain, which then produces an electromagnetic wave that can be picked up by others who are attuned to it. This explains why we sometimes have a gut feeling or sense that someone is thinking about us even without any physical contact or communication.

Intuitive telepathy has the power to transcend physical barriers and connect us with others regardless of distance. This has been observed in studies of twins, where they have been known to communicate telepathically even when they are miles apart. It has also been reported in cases of near-death experiences, where people claim to have communicated with loved ones who have passed away.

But beyond its scientific explanations, the power of intuitive telepathy lies in its ability to foster deeper connections and understanding between individuals. In a world where communication is often hindered by language barriers, cultural differences, and personal biases, intuitive telepathy offers a way for us to truly understand each other on a deeper level.

When we communicate through words, there is always room for misinterpretation and misunderstanding. We all have different levels of vocabulary, tone, and body language that can affect how our message is received by others. But with intuitive telepathy, there is no room for miscommunication because we are communicating through our thoughts and emotions which are universal and innate to all of us.

This form of communication also allows us to tap into the collective consciousness or the universal mind. The collective consciousness is a concept in psychology first introduced by Carl Jung, which suggests that there is a shared pool of knowledge and experiences that we all have access to. Through intuitive telepathy, we can tap into this collective consciousness and gain insights and wisdom beyond our individual understanding.

Intuitive telepathy also has the potential to enhance our relationships and connections with others. When we are able to communicate with someone on an intuitive level, it creates a sense of closeness and understanding that goes beyond words. It allows us to empathize with others and see things from their perspective, leading to stronger bonds and deeper relationships.

Moreover, intuitive telepathy can also be a powerful tool in resolving conflicts and promoting peace. In situations where verbal communication may be challenging or impossible, intuitive telepathy can offer a way for individuals to express their thoughts and emotions without the fear of judgment or misunderstanding. It allows for a more honest and open exchange of ideas, leading to mutual understanding and resolution.

So, how can we tap into our intuitive telepathic abilities? Like any skill, it takes practice and openness. One way to develop this ability is through meditation. By quieting our minds and focusing on our thoughts and emotions, we can become more aware of our own intuitive signals and learn to tune into others as well.

It is also essential to cultivate our intuition through self-awareness and mindfulness. By being more in tune with our thoughts, emotions, and surroundings, we can strengthen our intuitive sense and be more receptive to the signals of others.

In conclusion, intuitive telepathy is a fascinating phenomenon that has the potential to transform our connections with others. While there is still much to be explored and understood about it, there is no denying its power to transcend language barriers, foster deeper understanding and empathy, and enhance our relationships. So the next time you have a gut feeling or sense a strong connection with someone without any words being exchanged, remember that it could be your intuitive telepathic abilities at work. Embrace it and see where it takes you in your journey of communication and connection with others.

@@@@

CHAPTER 7

EMOTIONAL TELEPATHY

Have you ever felt like you could sense someone's emotions without them even saying a word? Or maybe you've experienced a strong connection with someone, where you can finish each other's sentences and know what the other is thinking or feeling? If so, then you may have experienced emotional telepathy.

Emotional telepathy, also known as emotional empathy or emotional intuition, is the ability to sense and understand the emotions of others without any verbal communication. It is a form of non-verbal communication that goes beyond words and actions, and instead relies on a deep understanding of emotions.

Although the concept of telepathy may seem far-fetched or even supernatural, there is scientific evidence to support the existence of emotional telepathy. Research has shown that humans have the ability to pick up on subtle cues and signals from others, allowing us to understand their emotions without any verbal communication.

So how does emotional telepathy work? It is believed that humans have a natural ability to read and interpret the emotional energy of others. This energy is often referred to as an aura or vibes, and it is constantly being emitted by our bodies. This energy can be picked up by our senses, allowing us to sense and understand the emotions of others.

One of the key factors in emotional telepathy is having a high level of emotional intelligence. Emotional intelligence is the ability to recognize, understand, and manage our own emotions as well as the emotions of others. Those with high levels of emotional intelligence are more likely to pick up on subtle cues and signals from others, making them more in tune with emotional telepathy.

But how exactly does one develop emotional intelligence and enhance their abilities in emotional telepathy? It all starts with self-awareness. Being aware of your own emotions and how they impact your thoughts and actions is crucial in understanding the emotions of others. By being more in tune with your own emotions, you can better understand and empathize with the emotions of others.

Another important aspect is being present and fully engaged in the moment. In today's fast-paced world, we are often distracted and not fully present in our interactions with others. This can hinder our ability to pick up on subtle emotional cues. By being present and actively listening to others, we can better understand their emotions and strengthen our emotional telepathy.

Practicing active listening also involves paying attention to non-verbal cues, such as body language and facial expressions. These non-verbal cues can often communicate more than words and can give insights into someone's true emotions. By being aware of these cues, we can better understand the emotions behind someone's words.

Another way to enhance emotional telepathy is through empathy. Empathy is the ability to understand and share the feelings of another person. By putting ourselves in someone else's shoes, we can gain a deeper understanding of their emotions and strengthen our emotional telepathy.

In addition to developing our own emotional intelligence, there are also techniques that can be used to improve our abilities in emotional telepathy. One such technique is visualization. This involves imagining yourself in someone else's situation and trying to feel what they might be feeling. This practice can help us become more attuned to the emotions of others and enhance our emotional telepathy.

Another technique is mindfulness meditation. This practice involves focusing on the present moment and being fully aware of our thoughts, emotions, and surroundings. By being more mindful, we can become more in tune with our own emotions as well as the emotions of those around us.

It is also important to note that while emotional telepathy can be a powerful tool for understanding and connecting with others, it should never be used to manipulate or control others. It is essential to respect boundaries and only use this ability for positive purposes.

So why is emotional telepathy important? For one, it can help us build stronger and more meaningful relationships with others. By understanding the emotions of those around us, we can better empathize and connect with them on a deeper level. It can also help us navigate tricky situations and conflicts by allowing us to understand where someone else is coming from.

In addition, emotional telepathy can also contribute to a more harmonious and compassionate society. By being more in tune with the emotions of others, we can become more understanding and empathetic towards different perspectives and beliefs. This can promote harmony and reduce conflicts in our personal and professional relationships.

In conclusion, emotional telepathy is a powerful tool that allows us to understand and connect with others on a deeper level. It relies on our ability to read and interpret the emotional energy of others, which can be enhanced through developing our emotional intelligence and practicing techniques such as visualization and mindfulness. By understanding the power of emotional telepathy, we can foster stronger relationships, promote empathy, and compassion, and create a more harmonious society. So, the next time you feel like you have a strong connection with someone, remember that it may be due to your ability to tap into their emotions through emotional telepathy.

@@@@

CHAPTER 8

MENTAL TELEPATHY

Telepathy, or the ability to communicate thoughts, ideas, and emotions without the use of verbal or physical cues, has been a topic of fascination for centuries.

From ancient civilizations to modern science fiction, the concept of mind-to-mind communication has captured the imagination of many. But is telepathy just a figment of our imagination or does it have a scientific basis? In this chapter, we delve into the world of mental telepathy and explore its possibilities.

What is Mental Telepathy?

Mental telepathy, also known as thought transference or mind-to-mind communication, is the ability to transmit and receive thoughts, feelings, and information from one mind to another without using any known sensory channels. This means that telepathy operates beyond the five senses and allows individuals to exchange information through a direct connection between their minds.

The term telepathy was coined by French educator and psychologist, Frederic W.H. Myers in 1882. It is derived from the Greek words tele, meaning "distant," and patheia, meaning "feeling" or "perception." The term was first used in a scientific context by British physicist Sir William Barrett in 1882.

Types of Mental Telepathy

There are two main types of mental telepathy – sender-initiated and receiver-initiated.

Sender-initiated telepathy occurs when an individual intentionally sends thoughts or messages to another person. This can be done through focused concentration or visualization techniques. The sender may also use a physical object or image as a medium to assist in the transmission of thoughts.

On the other hand, receiver-initiated telepathy occurs when an individual unexpectedly receives thoughts or messages from another person without any prior knowledge or conscious effort. This type of telepathy is often referred to as *"mind reading"* and can be experienced in various forms, such as sensing emotions, hearing words or phrases, or seeing images.

The Possibilities of Mental Telepathy

The concept of mental telepathy has been met with skepticism by many, but there have been numerous reported cases and studies that suggest its existence. Let's explore some of the potential applications and implications of mental telepathy.

1. Communication with Non-Verbal Individuals

One of the most exciting possibilities of mental telepathy is its potential to enable communication with non-verbal individuals, such as those with severe physical disabilities or those in a coma. This could greatly improve the quality of life for individuals who are unable to communicate through traditional means.

2. Enhancing Interpersonal Relationships

With telepathy, individuals can communicate their thoughts and emotions directly to their loved ones without any barriers. This could lead to a deeper understanding and connection between people, eliminating misunderstandings and conflicts caused by miscommunication.

3. Advancements in Education

Telepathy could revolutionize the way we learn and teach. Imagine being able to transmit knowledge directly from one mind to another without the need for textbooks or lectures. This could greatly enhance the learning experience and make education more efficient.

4. Assistance in Criminal Investigations

In law enforcement, telepathy could potentially assist in gathering valuable information from witnesses or suspects. This could also help in solving cold cases where traditional methods have failed.

The Scientific Evidence

While the idea of mind-to-mind communication may seem far-fetched, there have been numerous studies that provide some evidence for its existence.

One study conducted by psychologist Daryl Bem in 2011 showed that individuals were able to anticipate erotic images before they were shown, indicating a form of precognition or future knowing. Another study by neuroscientist *Dr. Jacobo*

Grinberg-Zylberbaum in 1994 demonstrated two subjects having synchronized brain waves when one of them was shown specific images, even though they were in different rooms.

Furthermore, there have been reported cases of identical twins and close relatives experiencing telepathic communication, suggesting a possible genetic component to telepathy.

Challenges and Limitations

While the potential of mental telepathy is exciting, there are also challenges and limitations that need to be considered. The biggest challenge being the lack of control over when and how telepathy occurs. It is not a skill that can be turned on and off at will, making it difficult to study and replicate in a controlled environment.

Additionally, the idea of mind-to-mind communication raises ethical concerns about privacy and consent. If telepathy were to become a widespread ability, it would require strict guidelines and regulations to ensure it is used responsibly.

Mental telepathy is a phenomenon that continues to intrigue and fascinate us. While there is still much to be discovered about its existence and potential applications, the evidence suggests that it may be a real and powerful ability. As we continue to delve into the mysteries of the human mind, we may one day unlock the full potential of mental telepathy and harness its possibilities for the betterment of humankind.

@@@@

CHAPTER 9

ASTRAL TELEPATHY

The concept of telepathy has fascinated humankind for centuries, with the idea of being able to communicate with others through thoughts and emotions without any physical means. While it may seem like a far-fetched concept, there is a form of telepathy that has been experienced and studied by many, known as Astral Telepathy.

Astral Telepathy is the ability to communicate with others through the astral plane, a dimension beyond our physical world where our consciousness can travel while we are in a state of deep relaxation or sleep. It is believed that during this state, our minds are more open and receptive to telepathic communication.

The concept of astral telepathy has been around for centuries, with mentions in ancient cultures such as the Egyptians and Greeks. However, it wasn't until the 19th century that it gained more attention and was studied by prominent figures such as Carl Jung and Sigmund Freud.

So how does astral telepathy work? It is believed that our thoughts and emotions emit energy waves that can be picked up by others in the astral plane. These energy waves act as a form of communication, allowing individuals to connect and exchange information without the use of words or physical gestures.

One of the main benefits of astral telepathy is the ability to communicate with loved ones who have passed away. It is believed that after death, our consciousness continues to exist in the astral plane, allowing us to connect with those who have crossed over. Many people have reported receiving messages or signs from their deceased loved ones through astral telepathy, bringing them comfort and closure.

Another benefit of astral telepathy is its potential for healing and self-discovery. By connecting with others in the astral plane, we can gain insights and perspectives that we may not have considered before. This can help us to understand ourselves better and make positive changes in our lives.

But how can one tap into astral telepathy? The first step is to achieve a state of deep relaxation or meditation. This can be done through techniques such as deep breathing, visualization, or guided meditations specifically designed for astral projection. It's important to clear your mind of any distractions and focus on your intention to communicate with others in the astral plane.

Once you have entered a state of deep relaxation, you can envision yourself traveling through the astral plane and connecting with others. It's important to keep an open mind and trust that you are capable of communicating telepathically. You may receive messages in the form of images, sensations, or even words in your mind.

It's worth noting that astral telepathy is not always accurate, as our thoughts and emotions can sometimes get in the way. It's essential to approach this practice with a sense of curiosity and not take everything at face value. Instead, use it as a tool for self-discovery and personal growth.

It's also essential to establish boundaries when practicing astral telepathy. Just as we have boundaries in our physical world, it's essential to respect the boundaries of others in the astral plane. This includes asking for permission before attempting to communicate with someone and respecting their decision if they do not wish to engage.

Some people may be skeptical about the concept of astral telepathy, and that is understandable. However, there have been numerous studies and experiments that support the existence of this phenomenon. In one study conducted by Dr. Stanley Krippner, two participants were able to successfully exchange information through telepathy while in the astral plane.

Furthermore, many individuals have reported experiencing astral telepathy without even trying, often during near-death experiences or during a state of extreme emotional distress. These experiences cannot be easily explained by science but suggest that there is more to our consciousness than what we currently understand.

In conclusion, the concept of astral telepathy may seem like something out of a science fiction movie, but it has been around for centuries and has been studied and experienced by many. Whether you believe in it or not, there is no denying the potential benefits and insights that can be gained from this practice. So why not try it and see what secrets of the astral plane you can unlock? Who knows, you may be surprised by what you discover.

@@@@

CHAPTER 10

TELEPATHY IN RELATIONSHIPS

The idea of being able to communicate with someone without saying a single word may seem like something out of a science fiction movie, but it's actually a real concept known as telepathy. Telepathy is the ability to communicate with another person using only your thoughts and feelings. While it may not be a widely accepted phenomenon, there are countless stories and experiences from people who believe in the power of telepathy, especially in the context of relationships.

In any relationship, communication is essential. It's how we express our wants, needs, and emotions, and it's how we connect with our partners. However, sometimes words can fall short and fail to convey the true depth of our feelings. This is where telepathy comes in – it allows us to connect with our partners on a deeper level, beyond spoken words.

One of the most significant benefits of telepathy in relationships is its ability to foster a sense of understanding and empathy between partners. When we can tune in to our partner's thoughts and emotions, we can better understand their perspective and see things from their point of view. This can help prevent misunderstandings and conflicts and promote a stronger emotional connection.

Telepathy also enables couples to communicate with each other even when they are physically apart. Whether it's due to distance or busy schedules, many relationships face the challenge of not being able to spend enough time together. In such cases, telepathy can be a powerful tool for staying connected. It allows couples to send each other supportive and loving thoughts throughout the day, creating a sense of closeness even when they are physically apart.

Moreover, telepathy can also help couples deepen their emotional intimacy. By being able to sense each other's thoughts and feelings, partners can open up and share their deepest fears, desires, and vulnerabilities without the fear of being judged or misunderstood. This kind of open and honest communication can bring a couple closer together and enhance their emotional bond.

But how can one develop and harness the power of telepathy in their relationship? It's essential to understand that telepathy is not a superpower that some people possess while others don't. It's a skill that can be cultivated and strengthened with practice. Here are some ways couples can develop telepathic communication in their relationship:

1. Practice Mindfulness

Mindfulness is the act of being fully present and aware of one's thoughts and feelings. It's an essential foundation for developing telepathy in relationships. By being mindful, partners can learn to quiet their minds and tune into each other's thoughts and emotions. This will help them become more receptive to each other's energy and strengthen their telepathic connection.

2. Meditate Together

Meditation is a powerful tool for developing telepathic abilities. By meditating together, couples can synchronize their brain waves, making it easier for them to tap into each other's thoughts and feelings. It also creates a peaceful and tranquil environment for couples to connect on a deeper level.

3. Use Visualization Techniques

Visualization is a technique that involves creating mental images of what you want to happen. Couples can use this technique to send each other loving and supportive thoughts while visualizing their partner receiving them. This will help strengthen their telepathic connection.

4. Pay Attention to Your Intuition

Intuition is our inner knowing or gut feeling, and it plays a significant role in telepathy. Couples can develop their intuition by paying attention to any subtle cues or signals from their partner. This will help them better understand each other's thoughts and feelings without the need for spoken words.

5. Communicate Openly

While telepathy may allow couples to communicate without spoken words, it's still essential to have open and honest communication in a relationship. Partners should regularly check in with each other and share their thoughts and feelings to strengthen their telepathic connection.

In addition to strengthening the bond between partners, telepathy can also help resolve conflicts in a relationship. When one partner is feeling upset or angry, the other can sense it through their telepathic connection. This allows them to address the issue before it escalates and causes further damage to the relationship.

However, like any other form of communication, telepathy can also have its challenges. For example, if one partner is more emotionally closed off or not receptive to their partner's energy, it can create a block in their telepathic connection. It's essential for both partners to be open, honest, and willing to work on developing their telepathic abilities together.

In conclusion, telepathy is a powerful tool that can significantly enhance a relationship. By allowing partners to connect on a deeper level and communicate beyond words, it can foster a stronger emotional bond and understanding between them. It also helps couples stay connected even when they are physically apart and resolve conflicts more effectively. If you're interested in exploring the power of telepathy in your relationship, start by practicing mindfulness and communicating openly with your partner. With time and dedication, you may be surprised at how strong your telepathic connection can become.

@@@@

CHAPTER 11

TELEPATHY IN BUSINESS RELATIONSHIPS

Business relationships are an integral part of any successful enterprise. Whether it's between colleagues, clients, or business partners, building and maintaining strong relationships is crucial for the growth and success of a company. While effective communication and networking skills are often emphasized in the business world, there is another aspect that is often overlooked – telepathy.

Telepathy, also known as mind-to-mind communication, is the ability to transmit and receive thoughts and feelings from one person to another without the use of physical communication. While some may dismiss telepathy as a pseudoscience or a concept reserved for science fiction, there is growing evidence and research suggesting that it plays a significant role in our daily lives, including our relationships in the business world.

In this chapter, we will explore the concept of telepathy and how it can be used to enhance and improve business relationships.

Understanding Telepathy

Telepathy has been a topic of fascination and speculation for centuries. It is believed that humans have the innate ability to communicate through thoughts, but it is often suppressed due to societal norms and conditioning. However, with the advancement of technology and a shift towards spiritual awakening, people are becoming more open to the idea of telepathy and its potential benefits.

In simple terms, telepathy can be described as communication through thoughts, emotions, or images without any verbal or physical exchange. It is a form of non-verbal communication that occurs on a subconscious level. It can happen between two individuals who share a close emotional connection or even between strangers who have a strong energetic bond.

The Role of Telepathy in Business Relationships

Now you may be wondering how telepathy relates to business

relationships. The truth is, telepathy can be a powerful tool in building trust, understanding, and effective communication with your colleagues, clients, and business partners. Here's how:

Enhances Empathy and Understanding

Empathy is the ability to understand and share the feelings of another person. In the business world, having empathy towards your colleagues and clients can help you build strong relationships and foster a positive work environment. Telepathy can enhance empathy by allowing you to tap into the thoughts and emotions of others, gaining a deeper understanding of their perspective and needs. This can help you anticipate their actions and respond accordingly, leading to better communication and cooperation.

Improves Non-Verbal Communication

In any relationship, non-verbal communication can often convey more than words can. Telepathy allows you to pick up on subtle cues and body language that may not be communicated verbally. This can be especially useful in negotiations, where understanding the other party's non-verbal cues can give you an advantage in the deal. By tuning into someone's thoughts and emotions, you can also gain insights into their true intentions, helping you make informed decisions.

Eases Tension and Conflicts

Misunderstandings, conflicts, and tension are common in any relationship, including business relationships. However, telepathy can help reduce such issues by facilitating a deeper understanding of others' perspectives. By being attuned to their thoughts and emotions, you can identify the root cause of conflicts and address them effectively before they escalate. This can lead to smoother communication and a more harmonious working relationship.

Strengthens Intuition

Intuition is often referred to as our "gut feeling" or "sixth sense."

It is our subconscious mind's way of communicating with us, providing insights or warnings about a situation or person. With telepathy, we can strengthen our intuition by being more in tune with our thoughts and emotions as well as those of others. This can be particularly useful in business relationships when making important decisions or judgments about someone's character or intentions.

How to Develop Telepathic Abilities

While some believe that telepathy is an innate ability, others argue that it can be developed through practice and training. Here are some ways you can strengthen your telepathic abilities:

Meditation:

Meditation helps quiet the mind and increase focus, making it easier to pick up on subtle thoughts and emotions. Regular meditation can also help you become more in tune with your own thoughts and feelings, making it easier to distinguish them from others.

Visualization:

Visualizing a strong, energetic connection between you and the person you want to communicate with can help strengthen telepathic communication. Imagine sending and receiving thoughts and feelings through this energetic bond.

Trust Your Intuition:

As mentioned earlier, our intuition is our subconscious mind's way of communicating with us. Trusting your intuition and acting upon it can help you develop and strengthen your telepathic abilities.

Practice with a Partner:

Find someone who is open to the concept of telepathy and practice sending and receiving thoughts and emotions with them. Start with simple exercises, such as guessing what the other person is thinking or sending simple messages.

In conclusion, telepathy may seem like a far-fetched idea in the business world, but its potential benefits cannot be ignored. By developing and utilizing telepathic abilities, we can enhance our relationships, improve communication, and gain a deeper understanding of others. So next time you're in a meeting or negotiating a deal, try tapping into your telepathic abilities – you may be surprised at the results!

@@@@

CHAPTER 12

TELEPATHY IN HEALING AND THERAPY

The human mind is a complex and powerful tool that has been the subject of fascination and study for centuries. It is through our minds that we can communicate, process information, and experience the world around us. But what if I told you that our minds are also capable of something much more extraordinary – telepathy.

Telepathy is the idea of being able to understand and communicate with someone without the use of words or any other form of communication. While this concept may seem far-fetched and supernatural to some, there is a growing body of evidence supporting the existence of telepathy and its potential use in healing and therapy.

The concept of telepathy has been around for centuries, with ancient cultures and civilizations believing in its existence and harnessing its power for healing and spiritual purposes. However, it was not until the late 19th century that telepathy began to gain attention from the scientific community. In 1882, the Society for Psychical Research was formed in London, with one of its main focuses being the study of telepathy. Since then, many studies have been conducted on telepathy, with many researchers claiming to have found evidence supporting its existence.

One area where telepathy has shown promise is in the field of healing and therapy. The idea that our thoughts and intentions can affect our physical well-being is not a new concept. The placebo effect, for example, is a well-known phenomenon where a person experiences a positive effect from a treatment simply because they believe it will work. This shows that our thoughts and beliefs have a powerful influence on our bodies.

In the same way, telepathy can be used as a tool for healing and therapy by harnessing the power of our minds to promote physical and emotional well-being. In fact, many alternative healing practices such as Reiki, acupuncture, and meditation are based on the principle of energy and intention being directed towards healing.

One example of telepathy being used in healing is through the practice of distant healing. This involves a healer sending positive thoughts, intentions, and energy towards a person who is not physically present. Studies have shown that distant healing can have a positive impact on a person's physical and emotional well-being, even when they are unaware that they are receiving this form of treatment.

Additionally, telepathy has also been used in therapy to enhance communication and understanding between a therapist and their client. By tapping into the thoughts and feelings of their client, a therapist can gain a deeper understanding of their struggles and provide more effective treatment.

One study conducted by researchers at the University of California found that telepathic communication between therapists and clients led to better outcomes in psychotherapy sessions. This was due to the therapist being able to address the root cause of the client's issues by accessing their subconscious thoughts and feelings.

Furthermore, telepathy has also been used in group therapy settings to promote empathy and understanding among participants. By allowing individuals to connect and communicate through their thoughts and emotions, group therapy sessions can be more impactful and transformative.

In addition to its potential use in healing and therapy, telepathy can also have a positive impact on our daily lives. It has the power to improve our relationships by fostering a deeper understanding and connection with others. It can also help us tap into our intuition and make better decisions based on our gut feelings.

However, it is important to note that telepathy, like any other skill, requires practice and proper guidance to be harnessed effectively. Just like how we train our bodies through exercise, we must also train our minds to develop this ability.

Some techniques that can help improve telepathic abilities include meditation, visualization, and energy work. These practices can help us clear our minds and focus our thoughts, making it easier for us to connect with others on a deeper level.

In conclusion, telepathy is a powerful tool that has the potential to greatly impact our lives, especially in the realms of healing and therapy. While it may still be considered a controversial concept by some, the growing body of evidence supporting its existence and potential applications cannot be ignored. As we continue to explore the depths of our minds and the power they hold, we may discover even more ways in which telepathy can be utilized for the betterment of ourselves and those around us.

@@@@

CHAPTER 13

SOME REAL-LIFE EXAMPLES OF TELEPATHY IN EVERYDAY LIFE

Telepathy, or the communication between minds without the use of any physical or verbal means, is a concept that has fascinated humankind for centuries. *While it was initially considered to be a supernatural ability, advancements in science and technology have shed light on the possibility of telepathy being a real phenomenon.* In fact, many people claim to have experienced telepathy in their daily lives, providing some intriguing real-life examples of this mysterious phenomenon. In this chapter, we will explore and discuss some of these examples to better understand the possibilities of telepathy in our everyday lives.

1. Twin Connection:

One of the most frequently cited examples of telepathy is the connection between twins. Twins are believed to have an unbreakable bond, and many twins claim to be able to communicate with each other telepathically. This connection is often described as an intense feeling or knowing what the other twin is thinking or feeling without any verbal or physical cues. Studies have also shown that twins tend to have similar thought patterns and can even finish each other's sentences, further supporting the idea of telepathic communication between them.

2. Animal Communication:

Telepathy is not limited to human beings; there are also numerous examples of telepathic communication between humans and animals. Many pet owners claim to be able to communicate with their pets telepathically, understanding their needs and desires without any verbal communication. This is especially common in cases where the pet is sick or injured and cannot express its needs through traditional means.

In some cases, animals have also been observed to display telepathic abilities among themselves. For instance, herd animals like elephants and whales have been witnessed communicating with each other over long distances through what is believed to be telepathic signals. These instances further demonstrate that telepathic communication may not be restricted to just human beings.

3. Mother-Child Bond:

The bond between a mother and child is often described as unbreakable, and telepathy seems to play a significant role in this relationship. Many mothers have reported being able to sense their child's needs, emotions, and even thoughts without any verbal communication. This is particularly common during the early stages of a child's life when verbal communication is limited.

In some cases, this telepathic connection has also been observed between adopted children and their biological mothers. The adopted children may have never met their biological mother, but they still feel a strong connection and are able to communicate with them telepathically.

4. Empathic Abilities:

Empathy, or the ability to understand and share the feelings of others, is intricately linked to telepathy. Some people possess empathic abilities that allow them to sense the emotions and thoughts of those around them without any verbal communication. This can be seen in instances where someone is able to accurately guess what someone else is thinking or feeling without any obvious cues.

Empathic abilities are common in caregivers, therapists, and other individuals who work closely with people. These individuals are more sensitive to the emotions of others, making it easier for them to notice telepathic signals.

5. Synchronicity:

Synchronicity is the occurrence of two events that are seemingly unrelated but happen at the same time and have a meaningful connection. While it may seem like a mere coincidence, some believe that synchronicity is a result of telepathic communication between individuals.

For example, you may be thinking about an old friend you have not spoken to in years, and suddenly they call you out of the blue. Or you may be struggling with a problem, and someone close to you suggests the exact solution you were thinking about. These instances of synchronicity hint at the possibility of telepathic communication between individuals.

6. Non-Verbal Communication:

Telepathy is often associated with communication between minds, but it can also manifest through non-verbal cues. Many people claim to have experienced telepathic communication with their loved ones through eye contact, hand gestures, or even facial expressions. This is especially common in close relationships where individuals have a deep understanding of each other's thoughts and feelings.

While these non-verbal cues may seem insignificant, they can convey a lot of information and create a telepathic connection between individuals.

In conclusion, these are just some of the real-life examples of telepathy in our daily lives. While there is still much debate and skepticism surrounding this phenomenon, these examples provide compelling evidence that telepathy may exist and play a role in our everyday interactions.

With advancements in technology and research, we may one day be able to fully understand and harness the power of telepathy. Until then, let us keep an open mind and continue to explore the possibilities of telepathic communication in our daily lives. Who knows, you may have experienced it without even realizing it.

@@@@

CHAPTER 14

THE EVOLUTION OF HUMAN CONCIOUSNESS

Since the dawn of human civilization, our species has been fascinated with the concept of telepathy - the ability to communicate with others through thoughts or feelings, without the use of verbal or physical cues. From ancient mythology to modern science fiction, telepathy has been a subject of intrigue and speculation. But as we continue to evolve as a species, could it be that our consciousness is also evolving, bringing us closer to the possibility of telepathic communication? In this chapter, we will explore the evolution of human consciousness and its potential connection to telepathy.

The concept of telepathy can be traced back to ancient civilizations, where it was often associated with supernatural or divine powers. In Hinduism, there is a belief in telepathic communication between gurus and their disciples, as well as between gods and mortals. In Greek mythology, there are tales of gods and goddesses communicating with each other telepathically. These early beliefs suggest that the idea of telepathy has been present in our consciousness for centuries.

As human civilization progressed, so did our understanding of the world around us. With the rise of science and technology, telepathy began to be seen in a different light - not as a supernatural ability, but as a potential scientific phenomenon. *In the late 19th and early 20th century, researchers such as Sigmund Freud and Carl*

Jung explored the concept of telepathy and its connection to the human psyche. They believed that telepathic abilities were deeply rooted in our subconscious minds, and that they could be accessed through techniques such as hypnosis and dream analysis.

However, it was not until the mid-20th century that scientific experiments were conducted to test the validity of telepathy. In

1935, J.B. Rhine at Duke University conducted a series of experiments on telepathy, popularly known as the *"Zener cards"* experiments. These experiments involved a sender and a receiver, where the sender would try to send a mental image to the receiver who would then try to guess the image. While the results were not conclusive, they did show some evidence of telepathic abilities.

Fast forward to the present day, and we see an increasing interest in the scientific community towards telepathy. With advancements in technology and brain research, scientists are now able to study the brain and its functions in greater detail than ever before. This has led to the discovery of mirror neurons - a type of brain cell that is believed to be responsible for empathy and our ability to understand and mimic the actions of others. Some researchers have suggested that these mirror neurons could also be the key to telepathic communication.

But what does all of this have to do with the evolution of human consciousness? To answer that question, we must first understand what consciousness is. Simply put, consciousness is our awareness of ourselves and the world around us. It includes our thoughts, feelings, perceptions, and emotions. It is believed that consciousness has evolved over millions of years, from simple organisms with basic survival instincts to complex beings with self-awareness.

As humans, our consciousness is constantly evolving and adapting to new challenges and environments. Our ability to communicate with verbal and non-verbal cues has played a crucial role in our evolution as a species. But could this evolution also include the development of telepathic abilities?

Some experts believe that as we continue to evolve, our consciousness is becoming more interconnected and attuned to each other. With the advancement of technology and communication, we are now more connected than ever before. We can instantly connect with people from various parts of the world through social media and video calls. This constant connection could be a contributing factor to the evolution of our consciousness towards telepathy.

Another theory suggests that as we become more technologically advanced, our need for physical communication and cues may decrease. This could lead to the development of other forms of communication, such as telepathy, to fill the gap. It is also possible that as our consciousness evolves, we may tap into the collective consciousness - a shared pool of knowledge and experiences that connects all human beings.

So, is telepathy a possibility in our future? *While there is no conclusive evidence to prove its existence, the evolution of human consciousness and the advancements in technology make it an intriguing possibility.* As we continue to explore and understand the complexities of our consciousness, perhaps one day we will unlock the mysteries of telepathy.

In conclusion, the concept of telepathy has been present in our consciousness for centuries, but it was not until recently that it has been explored scientifically. The evolution of human consciousness and its potential connection to telepathy is a subject of ongoing research and speculation. As we continue to evolve as a species, who knows what the future holds for our ability to communicate with each other through thoughts and feelings alone. One thing is for sure - the evolution of human consciousness and its potential for telepathy is a fascinating topic that will continue to captivate our minds for years to come.

@@@@

CHAPTER 15

DEVELOPING TELEPATHIC ABILITIES

Telepathy, the ability to communicate with others through thoughts and feelings without the use of words or physical gestures, has long been a topic of fascination and speculation. From ancient myths and legends to modern science fiction, the concept of telepathy has captured our imagination and sparked our curiosity.

But what if I told you that telepathy is not just a myth or a work of fiction? What if I told you that it is a real, innate ability that every human possesses to some degree? In this chapter, we will explore the world of telepathy and dive into the steps you can take to unlock and develop your own telepathic abilities.

Understanding Telepathy

Before we dive into the development of telepathic abilities, it is important to understand what exactly telepathy is and how it works.

Telepathy, also known as mind-to-mind communication or extrasensory perception (ESP), is the ability to transmit thoughts, emotions, or sensations from one individual to another without using any known physical or sensory channels. It is often described as a form of nonverbal communication that occurs between two minds.

While there is still much debate and skepticism around the existence of telepathy, there have been numerous studies and experiments that suggest its validity. For example, in 2014, a team of neuroscientists from Harvard University published a study in which they were able to use brain-computer interfaces to transmit simple messages directly from one person's brain to another's.

Furthermore, many people have reported experiences of telepathy in their daily lives, such as thinking of someone and then receiving a call or message from them. It is believed that we all possess some degree of telepathic ability, but it often goes unnoticed or undeveloped due to societal norms and lack of awareness.

Developing Your Telepathic Abilities

Just like any other skill, developing telepathic abilities requires practice, patience, and dedication. It is not a quick or easy process, but with consistent effort, you can tap into the power of your mind and unlock your full telepathic potential.

1. Enhance Your Mental Awareness

The first step in developing telepathic abilities is to enhance your mental awareness. This means being more conscious and mindful of your thoughts and feelings, as well as those of others. Start by practicing meditation and mindfulness exercises to quiet your mind and improve your focus. This will help you to tune in to your inner thoughts and emotions, as well as those of others.

2. Connect with Your Intuition

Intuition is often described as our inner voice or gut feeling that guides us in decision-making. It is also closely linked to telepathy, as both involve tapping into our subconscious mind. To develop your telepathic abilities, it is important to trust your intuition and learn to differentiate between your own thoughts and external messages.

3. Practice Visualization Techniques

Visualization is a powerful tool for developing telepathy. By visualizing yourself sending and receiving messages with another person, you are training your mind to make that connection.

Start by visualizing simple messages like colors or shapes, then gradually move on to more complex messages.

4. Strengthen Your Empathy

Empathy, the ability to understand and share the feelings of others, is a key component of telepathy. By strengthening your empathy, you are better able to sense the emotions of others and communicate with them on a deeper level. Practice putting yourself in other people's shoes and truly listening to their thoughts and feelings.

5. Experiment with Telepathy Exercises

There are many exercises and games that can help you develop your telepathic abilities. One popular exercise involves having two people sit facing each other and attempting to guess what the other person is thinking. Another exercise involves sending and receiving images or messages while in a relaxed state.

6. Trust Your Progress

It is important to trust your progress and not get discouraged if you do not see immediate results. Developing telepathic abilities takes time and effort, and everyone's journey is unique. Be patient with yourself and trust that with consistency, your skills will continue to improve.

Benefits of Developing Telepathic Abilities

Aside from the potential for mind-blowing communication, there are many other benefits to developing your telepathic abilities.

1. Improved Communication

Telepathy can greatly enhance communication between individuals, as it allows for a deeper understanding and connection. It can also be useful in situations where verbal communication is not possible, such as in a noisy environment or with someone who is nonverbal.

2. Enhanced Intuition and Empathy

As mentioned earlier, telepathy is closely linked to intuition and empathy. By developing your telepathic abilities, you will also strengthen these skills, leading to better decision-making and deeper connections with others.

3. Increased Mindfulness and Mental Clarity

Practicing telepathy requires a high level of mental awareness and focus, which can lead to improved mindfulness and mental clarity. You will become more in tune with your thoughts and emotions, as well as those of others, leading to a greater sense of self-awareness.

4. Strengthened Relationships

Telepathy has the power to deepen relationships by fostering a stronger understanding and connection between individuals.

It can also help resolve conflicts by enabling better communication and empathy.

Telepathy may, therefore, seem like a mystical concept, but it is actually a natural ability that we all possess to some degree. By following these steps and dedicating yourself to consistent practice, you can unlock and develop your own telepathic abilities. Not only will this enhance your communication skills, but it can also lead to a deeper understanding and connection with others. So, why not tap into the power of your mind and see what telepathy can do for you?

@@@@

CHAPTER 16

THE ROLE OF INTUITION IN TELEPATHY

Telepathy, the ability to communicate with another person without the use of physical or verbal cues, has long fascinated and mystified people. From ancient spiritual practices to modern science, telepathy has been explored and theorized about in various ways. One aspect that is often associated with telepathy is intuition. But what is the role of intuition in telepathy? Is it just a mere coincidence or is there a deeper connection between the two? Let us dive into this intricate topic and try to understand the relationship between intuition and telepathy.

Intuition, often referred to as our *"sixth sense,"* is a phenomenon that has been experienced by humans for centuries. It is the ability to understand something instinctively, without the need for conscious reasoning. Some people believe that intuition is a form of extrasensory perception (ESP) and is closely linked to telepathy.

Telepathy is often portrayed in science fiction as a way of communicating with others through a mind-to-mind connection. While telepathy has not been scientifically proven, there are many anecdotal accounts of people experiencing it in various forms.

The Role of Intuition in Telepathy:

The exact mechanism behind telepathy is still unknown, but many experts believe that intuition plays a crucial role in this phenomenon. In order to understand this connection, we first need to look at how intuition works.

Intuition is often described as a gut feeling or a sensation that comes from within. It is an unconscious process that allows us to tap into our inner knowledge and make decisions based on instinct rather than logical reasoning. Our intuition can notice subtle cues and information that we may not consciously be aware of, leading us to make accurate predictions or judgments.

In telepathy, intuition is believed to work in a similar way. It is said that telepathic individuals possess a heightened sense of intuition, which allows them to notice the thoughts and feelings of others. This can happen even if the other person is not physically present and can occur across vast distances.

The Role of Intuition in Receiving Telepathic Messages:

When it comes to telepathy, intuition plays a significant role in receiving messages from others. It is said that telepathic communication occurs through the transfer of energy between individuals. The sender sends out a message telepathically, and the receiver picks up on this message through their intuition.

Intuition helps the receiver to interpret and decode these telepathic messages. As mentioned earlier, intuition can pick up on subtle cues and information that we may not be consciously aware of. This ability becomes especially crucial in telepathy as it allows the receiver to understand and make sense of the incoming messages.

The Role of Intuition in Sending Telepathic Messages:

While receiving telepathic messages may rely heavily on intuition, sending telepathic messages also requires a certain level of intuition. In order to send a message telepathically, one needs to be able to focus their thoughts and emotions with great precision. Intuition plays a vital role in this process as it helps the sender to tune into their own inner knowledge and channel it towards the intended recipient.

Moreover, it is believed that individuals who have a strong connection with their intuition are better at telepathic communication as they can better control their thoughts and emotions, making their messages clearer and stronger.

The Connection Between Intuition, Telepathy, and Empathy:

Another interesting aspect to consider when discussing the role of intuition in telepathy is the connection between empathy and telepathy. Empathy is the ability to understand and share the emotions of others. It is closely linked to intuition as it also involves noticing subtle cues and information from others.

It is believed that individuals who are highly empathetic also tend to have a stronger intuition, making them more receptive to telepathic communication. This is because empathy and intuition both require individuals to be highly attuned to their own emotions, as well as others' emotions.

The Limitations of Intuition in Telepathy:

While intuition plays a significant role in telepathy, it is important to note that it is not the only factor at play. Intuition may help us to pick up on telepathic messages, but it cannot always guarantee the accuracy or clarity of these messages. Other factors such as our own biases, emotions, and distractions can also affect the transmission and reception of telepathic messages.

Moreover, telepathy is a complex phenomenon that involves both the sender and receiver being able to tap into their own intuition and energy. It requires a strong connection and synchronization between both parties, which may not always be possible.

In conclusion, the role of intuition in telepathy is still a subject that is open to much speculation and debate. While there is no scientific evidence to support the existence of telepathy, many believe that intuition plays a crucial role in this phenomenon. Intuition allows us to tap into our inner knowledge and connect with others on a deeper level. Whether or not telepathy truly exists, one thing is for sure – our intuition will always play an essential role in our understanding of ourselves and the world around us.

@@@@

CHAPTER 17

TELEPATHY AND THE UNIVERSE

The concept of telepathy has fascinated humans for centuries. The idea of being able to communicate with others through thoughts and emotions without any physical or verbal means is truly intriguing. While many may dismiss it as mere science fiction, there are those who firmly believe in the existence of telepathy and its connection to the vast expanse of the universe.

Telepathy is believed to be a form of extrasensory perception (ESP) that allows individuals to receive and transmit thoughts, feelings, and sensations.

But how does telepathy tie into the universe? The answer lies in the interconnectedness of all things in the universe. According to quantum physics, everything in the universe is connected through a web of energy and information, known as the quantum field. This field is responsible for creating and maintaining the fabric of reality, and it is believed that telepathy is one way to tap into this field and communicate with others.

The idea of telepathy and its connection to the universe is not a new one. Ancient civilizations such as the *Egyptians, Greeks, and Native Americans* all had beliefs and practices centered around telepathic communication. They understood that everything in the universe is connected, and they harnessed this connection for various purposes.

In modern times, there have been numerous reported cases of telepathy and its effects on individuals. One famous example is that of twin siblings who claimed to have a telepathic connection since birth. Researchers have also conducted studies on telepathy, with some yielding positive results. For instance, in a 2017 study published in the Journal of Neuropsychology, researchers found that twins had a more significant correlation in their brain activity than non-twin siblings, suggesting a potential telepathic connection.

But how does telepathy work, and how can we tap into this seemingly mystical ability? The truth is, the mechanics of telepathy are still largely unknown and are often subject to debate. Some theories suggest that telepathy works through the use of brain waves or electromagnetic signals. Others believe it is a form of advanced intuition or empathy.

One theory that has gained traction in recent years is the concept of quantum entanglement. This phenomenon occurs when two particles become entangled and share a connection regardless of distance. Scientists have observed this phenomenon in the subatomic world, and some believe that it could also apply to humans. In other words, if we consider ourselves as a collection of particles, it is possible that we are all entangled with each other, allowing for telepathic communication.

The idea of telepathy and its relation to the universe raises questions about the limits of our reality. Could we communicate with beings from other planets or dimensions through telepathy? Is it possible to tap into the collective consciousness of the universe and gain knowledge from it? These are all intriguing possibilities that challenge our current understanding of the universe.

Some may argue that telepathy is nothing more than a figment of our imagination, but there are those who believe that it holds immense potential for humanity. Imagine a world where we can communicate without barriers, where language and cultural differences no longer divide us. Telepathy could also be used to enhance our understanding of ourselves and others, leading to more profound connections and relationships.

However, as with any extraordinary ability, there are ethical concerns surrounding telepathy. The invasion of privacy and lack of consent are two major issues that must be addressed before fully embracing the concept of telepathy. As with any advancement in science and technology, there must be responsible use and proper guidelines in place to ensure the well-being of individuals.

In conclusion, the concept of telepathy and its connection to the universe is a fascinating one that has been explored by various cultures throughout history. While its existence and mechanics may still be subject to debate, there is no denying the endless possibilities that telepathy presents for humanity. It challenges our understanding of the universe and forces us to question the limits of our reality. Whether telepathy is a real phenomenon or not, one thing is for sure – it has captured our imaginations and will continue to do so for generations to come.

@@@@

CHAPTER 18

THE ETHICS OF TELEPATHY

The idea of being able to read someone's mind or transmit one's own thoughts without speaking a single word is both intriguing and unsettling. While telepathy may still be considered a concept of science fiction, advancements in technology and neuroscience have made it a possibility in the near future. As this potential becomes more tangible, it is important to consider the ethics and values that come with the ability to read and manipulate another person's thoughts.

The first question that comes to mind is whether telepathy would be an invasion of privacy. In a world where thoughts are no longer private, individuals would not have the freedom to keep their innermost feelings and thoughts to themselves. This raises concerns about personal autonomy and the right to mental privacy. With telepathy, there is a risk of constantly being monitored and judged based on one's thoughts rather than actions. This could lead to a society where people are fearful of their own thoughts and censor themselves constantly, ultimately hindering their personal growth and development.

Furthermore, telepathy can also potentially be used as a tool for manipulation and control. Just like any other form of communication, telepathy can be used to influence others and sway their decisions. This could be especially dangerous in the wrong hands, where individuals with ill intentions could manipulate others for personal gain or to cause harm. The power dynamics in relationships would also be altered with the ability to read one's partner's mind. Trust could easily be broken if one person knows everything the other is thinking, leading to potential abuse and exploitation.

Another ethical concern is the potential for discrimination and bias in telepathic communication. Our thoughts are shaped by our experiences, beliefs, and biases, which can lead to stereotyping and discrimination. If telepathy is used to make decisions about others, it could perpetuate these biases and deny individuals opportunities based on their thoughts rather than their actions and character. This could also lead to the marginalization of minority groups who may have different thought patterns that go against societal norms.

In addition, *telepathy can raise concerns about consent. In a world where thoughts can no longer be kept private, individuals would have to give consent for their thoughts to be read or transmitted.* But what happens if someone refuses to give consent? Would they still be forced to participate in telepathic communication? These are important questions to consider when discussing the ethics of telepathy.

On the other hand, *some argue that telepathy could also have positive ethical implications. It could potentially enhance empathy and understanding between individuals by allowing them to truly understand each other's thoughts and feelings.* This could lead to more compassionate and empathetic relationships, ultimately promoting a more harmonious society. Telepathy could also have practical applications in fields such as medicine, where doctors could better understand their patients' pain and experiences, leading to more exact diagnoses and treatments.

Moreover, telepathy could also have significant ethical implications in the justice system. With the ability to read one's thoughts, it could potentially help in solving crimes and preventing wrongful convictions. However, this raises concerns about the right to a fair trial and the potential misuse of such information by law enforcement.

When discussing the ethics and values of telepathy, it is also important to consider the role of technology. While advancements in technology may make telepathy possible, it also raises concerns about its regulation and potential misuse. Will there be laws in place to protect individuals from having their thoughts read without consent? How will the data collected from telepathic communication be stored and used? These are important ethical considerations that must be addressed before telepathy becomes a reality.

In addition to ethical concerns, telepathy also raises questions about the values and morals that would shape a society where thoughts are no longer private. Would honesty and transparency become more valued, or would individuals become even more guarded and selective about the thoughts they share? Would empathy and understanding become more prevalent, or would manipulation and control dominate telepathic communication?

Ultimately, the ethics and values of telepathy are complex and multifaceted. While it could have many potential benefits, it also poses significant ethical concerns that must be carefully examined before its implementation. As with any new technology, it is essential to consider not only its potential benefits but also its potential harm and the measures that must be taken to ensure its ethical use.

The concept of telepathy may seem like an exciting and futuristic idea, but its ethical implications cannot be ignored. It raises important questions about personal autonomy, privacy, manipulation, bias, consent, and the role of technology in regulating such abilities. As we continue to make advancements in technology and neuroscience, it is crucial to have these discussions and consider the ethics and values that will shape a society where thoughts are no longer private.

@@@@

CHAPTER 19

TELEPATHIC COMMUNICATION IN THE FUTURE

Imagine a world where communication is no longer limited by language barriers, technological devices, or physical distance. A world where thoughts and emotions can be transmitted and received instantaneously, without the need for any external tools. This may seem like a concept straight out of a science fiction movie, but with the rapid advancements in technology and our understanding of the human brain, telepathic communication could become a reality in the near future.

While there have been many claims of telepathic communication throughout history, it has always been met with skepticism and dismissed as pseudoscience. However, recent studies and developments in neuroscience have shed new light on the possibility of telepathy being a real phenomenon.

Scientists have been studying the brain's ability to communicate through electrical signals for decades. They have made significant progress in understanding how our brains process thoughts and emotions and how these signals can be translated into words and actions. These developments have paved the way for telepathic communication to be considered a serious possibility.

One of the most promising breakthroughs in telepathy research has been the development of **Brain-Computer Interfaces (BCIs)**. These are devices that can read and interpret brain activity to control external objects or communicate with other devices. BCIs have been used successfully to help people with disabilities communicate and control prosthetic limbs. However, researchers are now exploring the potential for BCIs to enable telepathic communication between individuals.

The idea behind using BCIs for telepathic communication is simple - our brains emit electrical signals when we think or feel something. These signals can be captured by BCIs and decoded into words or images that can be transmitted to another person's brain. In essence, this would allow two individuals to communicate directly with their thoughts, bypassing the need for spoken or written language.

But how exactly would this work in practice? One possible scenario could involve wearing a small BCI device on your head, similar to a headset or a band. This device would constantly monitor your brain activity and interpret your thoughts and emotions. The information would then be transmitted wirelessly to another person's BCI device, allowing them to experience your thoughts and feelings in real-time.

The potential applications of telepathic communication are endless. From improving communication between people of different languages to enhancing teamwork and collaboration in the workplace, the possibilities are revolutionary. Imagine being able to truly understand what someone is thinking and feeling, without the limitations of verbal or non-verbal cues. This could lead to improved relationships, empathy, and understanding among individuals.

In addition to interpersonal communication, telepathy could also have significant implications in the fields of healthcare and education. BCIs could be used to help individuals with speech or motor disabilities communicate more effectively and independently. It could also revolutionize education by allowing students to learn directly from their teachers' thoughts and experiences.

Of course, as with any new technology, there are ethical concerns that need to be addressed. The idea of having our thoughts and emotions decoded and transmitted wirelessly can be unsettling for many. There are concerns about privacy, security, and the potential for misuse of this technology. It is crucial that these concerns are addressed before telepathic communication becomes widely available.

Another major obstacle in the development of telepathic communication is our limited understanding of the brain. While we have made significant progress in decoding brain signals, we are still far from fully understanding how the brain works. There is much more research and experimentation needed before this technology can become a reality.

Despite these challenges, the potential for telepathic communication is too significant to ignore. With continued advancements in technology and neuroscience, we may one day witness a world where telepathy is a norm rather than a fantasy. The implications of this breakthrough are truly mind-boggling and could have a profound impact on our society.

With the rapid advancements in technology and our understanding of the human brain, it may not be long before telepathy becomes a reality. The potential applications and implications of this breakthrough are vast, and it could revolutionize the way we communicate and interact with each other. While there are still many challenges to overcome, the future of telepathic communication is looking bright, and it may just be the next big leap in human evolution.

@@@@

CHAPTER 20

THE GLOBAL IMPLICATIONS OF TELEPATHY

Telepathy, the ability to communicate thoughts and feelings without any physical or verbal means, has always been a subject of fascination and speculation. Many consider it to be a part of science fiction, but recent advancements in technology and neuroscience have brought this concept closer to reality. With the potential of telepathy becoming a reality, it is important to understand the global implications of this phenomenon.

The idea of telepathy has been around for centuries, with mentions in ancient mythology and folklore. It has also been a popular topic in science fiction literature and films. However, *in recent years, researchers have made significant progress in understanding the mechanisms behind telepathy and developing technologies that can facilitate it.*

One of the most significant implications of telepathy is its potential to revolutionize communication. Imagine being able to communicate with anyone in the world instantly and without any barriers of language or distance. This could bridge the gap between nations, cultures, and individuals, leading to better understanding and cooperation among people.

In a globalized world, where communication is key to success and progress, telepathy could significantly impact various sectors such as business, education, healthcare, and diplomacy. For instance, in business, telepathic communication could facilitate real-time negotiations and decision-making processes between parties from different parts of the world. In education, students could learn from the best teachers regardless of their physical location. In healthcare, doctors could diagnose and treat patients remotely with the help of telepathic communication.

The potential of telepathy to enhance human connections also has social implications. With telepathy, people could share their thoughts and feelings directly with each other, leading to deeper emotional bonds and understanding. It could also reduce misunderstandings caused by miscommunication and promote empathy and compassion among individuals.

However, along with its benefits, telepathy also raises ethical concerns. The invasion of privacy is one of the biggest concerns associated with telepathy. If telepathy becomes a reality, individuals may have their thoughts and feelings accessed without their consent, leading to a violation of their right to privacy. This could also be a potential tool for manipulation and control, threatening the autonomy and free will of individuals.

Another ethical concern is the potential misuse of telepathic technology. With the ability to influence thoughts and feelings, it could be used for nefarious purposes such as mind control or espionage. This raises questions about the need for strict regulations and ethical guidelines regarding the development and use of telepathic technology.

As telepathy has the potential to break down barriers and bring people closer, it could also have a significant impact on cultural and societal norms. With the ability to directly share thoughts and feelings, there may be a shift towards a more open and inclusive society. However, this could also lead to a loss of individuality and privacy in certain cultures and societies that value these aspects.

Telepathy also has implications for religion and spirituality. Many religions have beliefs about telepathic communication with a higher power or spiritual entities.

If telepathy becomes a reality, it could challenge these beliefs and potentially change the way people perceive religion and spirituality.

Moreover, the global implications of telepathy extend beyond human interactions. It could also have an impact on our environment and natural resources. With improved communication, there may be more efficient use of resources and better coordination in addressing global issues such as climate change.

While telepathy is still in its early stages of development, the potential global impact of this phenomenon cannot be ignored. As with any technological advancement, there are both positive and negative implications that need to be carefully considered.

For telepathy to have a positive impact on society, it is crucial to address the ethical concerns surrounding its development and use. Stricter regulations and ethical guidelines must be in place to protect the privacy and autonomy of individuals. Research should also focus on understanding the potential long-term effects of telepathy on society, culture, and human psychology.

The concept of telepathy has intrigued humans for centuries, and with recent advancements in technology, it may soon become a reality. Its potential to revolutionize communication, enhance human connections, and address global issues is immense. However, it also raises ethical concerns that must be addressed. As we continue to explore and develop this phenomenon, it is important to carefully consider its global implications and take necessary precautions to ensure its responsible and ethical use.

@@@@

CHAPTER 21

UNLOCKING THE FULL POTENTIAL OF TELEPATHY

Telepathy, the ability to communicate using only the power of the mind, has long been a topic of fascination and intrigue. From science fiction novels to movies, telepathy has captured the imagination of people for centuries. But what if I told you that telepathy is not just a figment of our imagination, but a real and powerful tool that we all possess? What if I told you that by unlocking its full potential, we could revolutionize the way we communicate and connect with others? In this chapter, we will delve into the concept of telepathy and explore how we can unlock its full potential to enhance our lives in ways we never thought possible. Telepathy can occur in various forms, from simple communication between two individuals to more complex group telepathy. It can also take place within close proximity or across vast distances. Some people may experience telepathy spontaneously, while others may learn to develop and control this ability.

The Power of Mind Communication

The ability to communicate through telepathy has immense potential to transform human interaction and relationships. By tapping into this power, we can break through the barriers of language and distance and truly understand each other on a deeper level.

Think of all the times when miscommunication or misunderstandings have caused conflicts in our personal or professional relationships. Often, this happens because words can be misinterpreted or emotions can be masked. With telepathy, there is no room for miscommunication as thoughts and feelings are transmitted directly, without the filter of language.

Imagine being able to communicate with someone who speaks a different language effortlessly, or being able to sense what your loved ones are feeling even when they are miles away. Telepathy has the potential to bridge the gap between individuals and create a deeper sense of understanding and empathy.

Unlocking the Full Potential of Telepathy

So how do we unlock the full potential of telepathy? Like any other skill, it requires practice, patience, and an open mind. Here are some ways in which we can develop and enhance our telepathic abilities:

1. Meditation and Mindfulness

Meditation is a powerful tool for developing telepathic abilities. By quieting our mind and focusing on our thoughts, we can better tune in to the thoughts and emotions of others. Mindfulness practices also help us become more aware of our own thoughts and feelings, allowing us to better understand and control our own mental energy.

2. Build a Stronger Connection with Others

Telepathy is all about connecting with others on a deeper level.

Building stronger relationships with those around us can strengthen our telepathic abilities. This can be achieved by actively listening, expressing empathy, and being more emotionally attuned to those we interact with.

3. Pay Attention to Your Intuition

Intuition is often seen as a form of telepathy. It is that "gut feeling" or inner voice that guides us in decision making. By paying attention to our intuition and trusting it, we can develop a stronger connection with our own thoughts and feelings, making it easier to pick up on the thoughts and feelings of others.

4. Practice Telepathy Exercises

There are many exercises that can help us enhance our telepathic abilities. One simple exercise is to sit facing a partner and try to send or receive thoughts without speaking. Another exercise is to visualize sending positive thoughts or intentions to someone and see if they can sense it. With practice, these exercises can help strengthen our telepathic connection with others.

Benefits of Unlocking Telepathy

Unlocking the full potential of telepathy can bring about numerous benefits in our personal and professional lives. Here are some ways in which telepathy can enhance our overall well-being:

1. Improved Communication and Relationships

As mentioned earlier, telepathy can help us understand and connect with others on a deeper level. This can lead to improved communication and stronger relationships, both personally and professionally. By being more attuned to the thoughts and feelings of others, we can also avoid misunderstandings and conflicts.

2. Increased Empathy and Understanding

Telepathy allows us to experience the thoughts and feelings of others, making us more empathetic and understanding towards them. This can lead to a more harmonious and compassionate society as we learn to truly see and feel from another's perspective.

3. Enhanced Intuition and Decision Making

Developing our telepathic abilities can also strengthen our intuition, allowing us to make better decisions in our personal and professional lives. By being more in tune with our own thoughts and feelings, we become better equipped to make choices that align with our true desires.

4. Expansion of Consciousness

Telepathy can also open the doors to a higher level of consciousness. By tapping into this innate ability, we can expand our understanding of the world around us and connect with the collective consciousness of humanity.

Telepathy is a powerful tool that has the potential to transform the way we communicate and connect with others. By unlocking its full potential, we can break through barriers, deepen our relationships, and gain a deeper understanding of ourselves and those around us. So, let's embrace this incredible ability within us and explore the power of mind communication.

@@@@

CHAPTER 22

THE EPILOGUE

After numerous chapters filled with information, anecdotes, and scientific evidence, it's time to wrap up the journey of exploring the world of telepathy. The book "Telepathy: The Silent Language of the Universe" has been a deep dive into the concept of telepathy, its history, its potential, and it's fascinating connection to the universe. As we reach the end of this book, let's take a moment to reflect on the key takeaways from this enlightening read.

First, we have learned that telepathy is indeed a real phenomenon. It is not just a mere figment of imagination, or something reserved for science fiction movies. The evidence presented in this book, from scientific experiments to personal experiences, all point towards the existence of telepathy. This ancient concept has stood the test of time and continues to intrigue scientists and researchers worldwide.

One of the most fascinating aspects of telepathy is its connection to the universe. We have explored how telepathy transcends distance and time, making it a truly universal language. From telepathic communication between humans to animals and even plants, telepathy knows no boundaries. The concept of interconnectedness and oneness is strongly reinforced through telepathy, as it allows us to tap into a collective consciousness that exists beyond our individual selves.

Moreover, we have also delved into the history of telepathy and its evolution over time. From ancient civilizations using telepathic communication for survival to modern-day research and studies, we have seen how telepathy has been an integral part of human existence. The book also sheds light on how this phenomenon has been suppressed and ridiculed in some societies, leading to it being shrouded in mystery and disbelief.

Another crucial takeaway from this book is the potential of telepathy. We have seen how telepathy can be used for healing, both physical and emotional, and for enhancing our psychic abilities. The book has explored various techniques and exercises to develop telepathic skills, making it a practical guide for those interested in exploring this realm. The power of telepathy has immense potential to bring about positive change in the world, and it is up to us to tap into it.

But like any other skill or ability, telepathy requires practice, patience, and an open mind. It cannot be mastered overnight or without effort. The book emphasizes the importance of meditation, mindfulness, and self-awareness in developing telepathic abilities. It also cautions against misusing this power and highlights the significance of ethical considerations when using telepathy.

One of the most significant takeaways from this book is the importance of belief in telepathy. As mentioned earlier, telepathy has faced skepticism and disbelief in some societies, leading to its suppression and lack of research. But as we have seen through various examples and studies, belief is a crucial element in the manifestation of telepathic abilities. It is essential to approach telepathy with an open mind and allow ourselves to be receptive to its potential.

On a more personal note, this book has also emphasized the importance of intuition and trusting our inner voice. Telepathy is often associated with gut feelings and hunches, which can guide us towards making better decisions in life. Learning to listen to our intuition can lead us towards a deeper understanding of ourselves and the world around us.

As we conclude this epilogue, it is worth mentioning that *"Telepathy: The Silent Language of the Universe"* is just the beginning of our journey into the world of telepathy. This book has provided us with a foundation for further exploration and understanding of this fascinating phenomenon. It has challenged our beliefs and expanded our perspectives, urging us to explore the depths of our consciousness and our connection to the universe.

The book *"Telepathy: The Silent Language of the Universe"* is a thought-provoking and eye-opening read. It has shed light on a concept that is often dismissed or ignored in mainstream society. The key takeaways from this book include the existence of telepathy, its universality, its potential, and the importance of belief and intuition. It has encouraged us to tap into our innate abilities and explore the vast possibilities that telepathy has to offer. So let us continue on this journey with an open mind, an open heart, and a willingness to embrace the power of telepathy.

@@@@

CHAPTER 23

FURTHER READING

Telepathy, also known as mind-reading or thought transference, has long been a topic of fascination for humans. The idea of being able to communicate with someone through thought alone is both intriguing and mysterious. While it may seem like something out of a science fiction novel, telepathy has actually been studied and researched for many years.

In this chapter, we will delve into the world of telepathy and explore the various resources and literature available on this fascinating subject.

History of Telepathy

The concept of telepathy dates back to ancient times, with mentions of it found in ancient

Greek and Egyptian texts. However, it wasn't until the late 19th century that telepathy began to be studied scientifically. In 1882, the Society for Psychical Research was founded in London, and one of their main areas of research was telepathy.

Since then, there have been numerous studies and experiments conducted on telepathy, with varying results. While some claim to have experienced telepathic abilities, others remain skeptical and attribute it to coincidences or other factors.

Types of Telepathy

There are two main types of telepathy - spontaneous and experimentally induced. Spontaneous telepathy occurs without any external factors or intentional efforts, while experimentally induced telepathy is studied in a controlled environment with specific protocols.

There are also different forms of telepathy, such as *clairvoyance* (the ability to see distant events or objects), *precognition* (the ability to see future events), and *retrocognition* (the ability to see past events). While these abilities are often associated with telepathy, they may also exist independently.

Resources on Telepathy

Thanks to advancements in technology and the growing interest in parapsychology, there is a wealth of resources available on telepathy. Here are some of the main sources of information and literature on telepathy:

1) Books:

There are several books written on telepathy, both by scientists and enthusiasts. Some of the most popular ones include **"Telepathy: The True Story of an Incredible Psychic Connection"** by *Rupert Sheldrake*, **"The Reality of ESP: A Physicist's Proof of Psychic Abilities"** by *Russell Targ*, and **"Mind to Mind: An Investigation into the True and False Relation of**

Thought Transference" by *William Barrett.*

2) Scientific Journals:

Many reputable scientific journals, such as the **Journal of Parapsychology** and the **Journal of Consciousness Studies**, publish articles and studies on telepathy. These journals follow strict peer-review processes, making the information reliable and credible.

3) Online Sources:

The internet is a treasure trove of information on telepathy. There are countless websites and chapters dedicated to discussing and exploring this topic. However, it is essential to be cautious when reading information from online sources, as not all of them may be credible.

4) Documentaries:

For those who prefer visual mediums, there are several documentaries available on telepathy. Some popular ones include **"The Hidden Mind"** and **"The Science of Psychic Communication,"** both available on streaming platforms like *Netflix* and *Amazon Prime*.

5) Conferences and Workshops:

There are many conferences and workshops held around the world that focus on parapsychology and telepathy. These events bring together experts in the field to discuss their research findings and share their knowledge with the public.

6) Organizations:

As mentioned earlier, the Society for Psychical Research is one of the oldest organizations dedicated to studying telepathy and other paranormal phenomena. Other notable organizations include the Parapsychological Association and the Rhine Research Center.

Literature on Telepathy

Apart from resources mentioned above, there is also an abundance of literature available on telepathy. Many fictional works, such as **"The Shining"** by *Stephen King* and **"The Chrysalids"** by *John*

Wyndham, feature telepathy as a central theme. These works, while not based on scientific research, can offer an imaginative and entertaining perspective on the topic.

Furthermore, many scientific studies and experiments have been published in literature over the years. For example, the famous **"Ganzfeld experiments"** conducted by parapsychologist *Charles*

Honorton and his team in the 1970s, which aimed to test the existence of telepathy, have been extensively documented in literature.

Challenges and Controversies

While there is a vast amount of information and literature available on telepathy, there are also challenges and controversies surrounding the topic. One of the main challenges is the difficulty in replicating results in experiments. Some studies have shown positive results, while others have not been able to replicate those results.

Another controversy surrounding telepathy is the lack of a scientific explanation for how it works. Skeptics argue that there is no evidence or logical explanation for telepathy and that it may simply be a result of coincidence or other psychological factors.

Telepathy, therefore, remains a fascinating topic that has been studied and debated for centuries. While there is a vast amount of information and literature available on the subject, it is still a highly debated and controversial topic in the scientific community.

Whether you are a skeptic or a believer in telepathy, exploring the various resources and literature available can provide a deeper understanding and appreciation for this mysterious phenomenon. Who knows, perhaps one day we will uncover the secret behind telepathy and unlock its full potential. Until then, let us continue to delve into this fascinating world with an open mind and an eagerness to learn.

Here's a concise list of reference materials on the topic of telepathy:

Books:

1. "The Conscious Universe" by Dean Radin
2. "Telepathy and the Etheric Vehicle" by Alice Bailey
3. "The Science of Telepathy" by J.B. Rhine

4. "Mind Reach: Scientists Look at Psychic Ability" by Russell Targ and Harold Puthoff

5. "The Psychic Pathway" by Jeffrey Mishlove

Research Papers:

1. "Telepathy: A Review of the Literature" by Chris Roe (2014)

2. "Neural Correlates of Telepathy" by Samuel Moulton and Stephen Kosslyn (2011)

3. "Anomalous Cognition in Ganzfeld and Remote Viewing Experiments" by Daryl Bem (2011)

4. "Telepathy and the Brain" by Michael Persinger (2010)

5. "The Neurobiology of Telepathy" by Stuart Hameroff (2007)

Online Resources:

1. The International Society for the Study of Psi (ISSPSI)

2. The Parapsychological Association (PA)

3. The Journal of Parapsychology (JOP)

4. The Journal of Nervous and Mental Disease (JNMD)

5. The Stanford Research Institute (SRI) International's Remote Viewing Program

Documentaries:

1. "The Secret Life of the Brain" (PBS, 2002)

2. "The Mind Reader" (BBC, 2006)

3. "Telepathy: The Hidden Language" (Smithsonian Channel, 2011)

4. "The Psychic Detectives" (Court TV, 2004)

5. "The Stargate Project" (History Channel, 2008)

Remember to approach these resources with a critical eye, considering both the scientific rigor and potential biases.

@@@@

Printed in Great Britain
by Amazon